British Library Cataloguing in Publication Data

Testa, Fulvio
    If you take a paintbrush.
    I. Title
    823'.914[J]   PZ7
    ISBN 0-86264-037-7

To Juliane

© 1983 by Fulvio Testa.
First published in Great Britain in 1983 by Andersen Press Ltd.,
19-21 Conway Street, London W.1.
Published in Australia by Hutchinson Group (Australia) Pty. Ltd.,
Richmond, Victoria 3121.
All rights reserved. Printed in Italy by Grafiche AZ. Verona.

If You Take a Paintbrush

A BOOK OF COLOURS

FULVIO TESTA

Andersen Press · London

Hutchinson of Australia

Yellow is the colour of the sun.

Blue is the colour of the sea.

Yellow and blue together make green.

Green is the colour of trees in springtime.

Orange is the colour of oranges.

Red is the colour of apples.
Nicholas's car is red too.

Purple is the colour of the sweater Nicholas got for his birthday. Purple is the flower he gives to Nancy.

Brown is the colour of chocolate.

Grey is the colour of the water when you take a bath.

This cat is black. Black is the colour of the night.

White is the colour of snow.

White is a piece of paper waiting for colours.